THE GREAT MID-LIFE CAREER SWITCH

First published in 2010 by
Infinite Ideas Limited
36 St Giles
Oxford, OX1 3LD
United Kingdom
www.infideas.com
Based on the book *Overcoming Redundancy*, published by Infinite Ideas, 2009

A CIP catalogue record for this book is available from the British Library

ISBN 978–1–906821–56–2

Brand and product names are trademarks or registered trademarks of their respective owners.

Cover designed by Baseline Arts Ltd, Oxford
Typeset by Sparks – www.sparkspublishing.com
Printed in Great Britain

TECHNICAL NOTE ABOUT
THE REDUNDANCY TRANSFORMATIONS STUDY

The Redundancy Transformations Study was a nationally representative online survey of 1,004 adults aged 18 and over who had experienced redundancy during their working lives. It was carried out by Alternative Futures Research Ltd in February and March 2009. The online sample was provided by Toluna. An earlier pilot phase of this research comprising 147 online interviews was also carried out with the help of One Life Live. Where respondents from this research survey are quoted in this book, names have been changed to protect their identities.

For more information contact Alternative Futures Research Ltd
www.alternativefutures.biz

THE GREAT MID-LIFE CAREER SWITCH

15 IMPORTANT TIPS TO HELP YOU CHANGE CAREERS AT HALF-TIME

GORDON ADAMS

infiniteideas

CONTENTS

Introduction   vi

1 Research other careers   1
2 Seek career guidance   4
3 Carry out a skills audit on yourself   7
4 Retrain for a new career   10
5 Increase your skill set   14
6 Start your own business   17
7 Buy a business franchise   22
8 Give yourself a fresh image   26
9 Be focused   29
10 Network to develop your connections   33
11 Find inspiration   37
12 Take voluntary work   40
13 Use an interim solution as a stepping stone   43
14 Create a portfolio career   45
15 Believe in yourself!   48

Useful contacts   52
Other helpful books from Infinite Ideas   54

INTRODUCTION

We live in challenging times. Once there was a time when you had a job for life. You began as an apprentice, learned a trade and followed it through with the same employer for life.

Then we entered an age where people had a career for life. People had many different jobs during their lifetimes. They worked for a variety of employers across different industries, but stayed on a single career path. Their whole lives were spent within the same general discipline, such as sales, marketing, finance, customer service, personnel and administration. All of their training during their lives was focused on helping them succeed in that specific career.

Today's world is much more fluid. We are living and working for longer. Many of us will live into our 80s and 90s. It now seems likely that many of us may not retire until 70, or even later. Nowadays the Great Mid-Life Career Switch is becoming increasingly common. Here, people jump from one career track onto a different track, which leads in a very different direction. For a growing number of people the middle of their lives will even see the emergence of parallel career tracks: a portfolio career in which an individual pursues several different part-time careers at the same time.

This book contains fifteen simple tips to help you with your Great Mid-Life Career Switch.

You are a multi-talented individual capable of doing many different things in your working life. We all are. You have the ability to move in many different directions with your career or careers, if you really want to make this happen.

Remember the words of Ralph Waldo Emerson:

'What lies behind us and what lies before us
are tiny matters compared to what lies within us'

Good luck with your Great Mid-Life Career Switch!

Gordon Adams
Author of *Overcoming Redundancy*

1 RESEARCH OTHER CAREERS

You know you'd like to do something different – but what? Doing your homework on other career options is a sensible step to take right now.

It's a common dilemma. You feel it is time for a change in your working life.

Perhaps your last job never really felt right for you. It just isn't (or wasn't) you. You're continuing to work in this job but thinking of moving on, or perhaps redundancy has prompted you into reappraising what you want to do in your life. This could be a turning point for you.

But what else can you do? What other careers are you equipped for? What other jobs might you be good at, if you had appropriate retraining? You need to start by taking a hard look at yourself: the things you enjoy doing and what you are good at. You also need to be candid with yourself about the things you don't enjoy doing and what you struggle with. This should begin to narrow down the search.

You also need to examine all the jobs you have carried out in your career until now. What aspects of the jobs appealed and what did you find difficult? Are there any obvious links between the jobs you did and job switches you might make right now? For instance, could the 'poacher turn gamekeeper' – could you switch from being a client to a supplier?

Could you use your interpersonal skills in a different environment? Hopefully this kind of thinking will narrow the search down.

There are three main ways you can research new careers.

Firstly, take professional advice. If you've just been made redundant and have received outplacement support, your outplacement company will probably have provided some career guidance coaching. If not, you might also choose to invest in help from private career counsellors. Alternatively the Careers Advice Service, funded by the government, offers simple and free careers advice. They may be helpful in identifying career directions and training courses for you to consider. The Careers Advice Service website also allows you to take an online skills and interests assessment. This helpful website also allows you to look at hundreds of job profiles telling you what various jobs are like, what qualifications are needed and what pay and working hours you can expect. It can be a good start point.

Secondly, do some detailed desk research. Harness the full power of the Internet and your nearest major public library. Look at published information by professional bodies and industry bodies to help you understand specific professions and roles. Locate articles that have been written about that particular career. Identify from the articles you read, and from press interviews, who the experts are in the field – at some point you may be able to meet them.

Thirdly, use your networking contacts. Speak to everyone you meet about the jobs they do now and what they have done in the past. Discover what led them into their particular careers, whether they enjoy it, what the upsides and the downsides are. What qualifications did they need to get in? How did they find their jobs? Write up your notes on any job you're attracted to and then research that job further on the Internet. Go back to your contact and ask if they can introduce you to anyone else who does that job. The more people you can speak to in your chosen career, the better your understanding will be of what it's really like. You can clarify whether it seems like a career you would do well in. The more contacts you build up within your chosen career, the easier it will be to hear about entry-level job opportunities. Work the grapevine! You may even be able to use your network contacts as a way to secure some freelance work. This is a great way to develop your understanding of that career. If you have the opportunity to shadow someone in that career for a day, seize it! It will help you to learn and become an example for you to quote. This will be a way of demonstrating your enthusiasm for the role to a future employer.

Do your homework. Get yourself good information on other careers and you can begin to make the right choices.

The key to getting any job is having up-to-date and relevant skills. If your chosen career requires retraining, make sure you get the best training you can. Always remember, though, that employers will see many candidates with similar qualifications, so look for anything to improve your case that is 'over and above' the standard candidate offering. You need to give yourself the edge in job interviews. It will impress an employer if you have clearly used your initiative: you've researched that career, attended exhibitions and seminars at your own expense, and you've met with other people in different companies who do this job already.

In a difficult economic climate, it is particularly hard to move into a totally new career. However, by researching it thoroughly, you will put yourself in the best position to succeed.

2 SEEK CAREER GUIDANCE

You're standing at a crossroads now. The problem may be that you don't know which way to go from here. You don't even know which destinations can be reached by following the different directions. If you feel uncertain, now is the time to seek professional career guidance.

According to many experts, the problem some people have is knowing where to start. A recent survey by One Life Live showed that more than a third of us would like to retrain for a new career but most of us don't know what career we'd like to retrain for! We know we want to take a new career direction, we're ready for a change, but don't really know what other careers would be appropriate. In the hands of a skilled careers adviser or coach, diagnostic tools like psychometric tests and Career Anchoring exercises can often help point the way forward.

What are the top priorities for you in your working life?

Career Anchoring was developed by Edgar Schein, one of the founders of modern organisational psychology. The idea behind it is that each of us has a particular orientation towards work, approaching it with a certain set of priorities and values. These are our 'Career Anchors' – they are what motivate us, what drive us on. For you, being fulfilled at work might be all about challenge or about dedication to a greater cause, while for others it might be about autonomy or technical competence.

Careers Advisers who use this technique sometimes discover that people have selected their current career for the wrong reasons. People find their responses in the workplace are incompatible with their true values. The result is that such people are unhappy and unproductive in their work. Do you feel that describes you in your current or most recent job? If so, career coaching sessions can help you identify your true Career Anchors and perhaps point you in a new direction. Discover the real you: someone whose chosen career in future is in tune with your true priorities and values.

'Career Anchoring worked for me' says Bob, one of the respondents on the Redundancy Transformations Study carried out by Alternative Futures. 'It takes around thirty minutes' preparation and then an afternoon shut away with your Careers Coach. You need to go somewhere quiet where you can really focus. A good coach will ask tough questions and challenge you. It certainly forced me to think about what I wanted for the next one, five and ten years, so I could build a plan towards my future!'

Growth itself contains the germ of happiness.
PEARL S. BUCK

Private Careers Advisers often use psychometric tests to help them understand you as an individual. This enables them to give you better advice. Myers Briggs is one of the commonly used psychometric tests where you complete a questionnaire about yourself. The scores that emerge classify you according to four dimensions: Extrovert versus Introvert, Intuition versus Sensing, Thinking versus Feeling, Judgement versus Perception. Clearly the right role for an extrovert who intuitively feels their way through life's decisions and likes to take snap decisions is going to be different to that for an introverted thinker who always carries out detailed analysis and is cautious before acting.

If you don't have access to a private Careers Adviser or a coach who you can trust, then now could be the right time to seek one out! A small investment in taking this step now could reap great dividends in the future. So how do you find a coach? Start by asking friends and former colleagues whether they know anyone they can recommend. If this doesn't help, approach professional bodies which represent different types of coaches, for example the Association for Coaching. Or make use of the matchmaking service offered by the Coaching Academy, the UK's largest training organisation for coaches. If you register your details on the Coaching Academy website, they'll try to put you in touch with a coach who meets your needs. As Kris Robertson, a Director at The Coaching Academy, says 'A coach can help you clarify goals and find the motivation to take action, especially during a time in which you are re-evaluating your life and future career direction.'

You'll find no lack of coaches out there. The key is to choose a coach who you trust, who can help you in the particular area you need to make progress. Make sure you will get on well at a personal level with your coach. With help, you'll go far!

A zero cost option would be to speak to the Careers Advice Service, the publicly-funded advice service. You can have an initial free guidance session over the phone with one of their career coaches and take an online skills check. This may help you make the right first moves.

You are probably capable of much more than you think you are: capable of working in a wide number of different roles and of pursuing different careers. You will probably become happier for taking on a new challenge and feeling you are growing as an individual. Take some advice from me: the first thing you need to do is to take some advice!

3 CARRY OUT A SKILLS AUDIT ON YOURSELF

A skills audit may help you. It helps you appreciate the variety of jobs you are capable of fulfilling. It breaks open any rigid definition of your potential that may be holding you back. It fuels your self-esteem by reminding you of all the talents you have.

You are a multi-talented individual. Don't deny it: we all are. Here in the UK, we are masters of modesty. Given a chance, we will be self-effacing. If people pay us a compliment, we are most likely to deny it.

Have we ever stopped to think how foolish that makes the person offering the compliment feel? So perhaps it is time for us to do something different and do it openly, honestly and thoroughly. It's time for us to admit to ourselves the wide range of skills and talents that we have.

To make sure you do this thoroughly, set aside a whole day for this task. If you take this exercise seriously it will certainly help you.

Get a sheet of paper and head it with the words 'Skills audit'. You need two columns – one for your core skills (the things you are particularly good at) and one for all the other skills you possess (some of which you might need to brush up on). Please don't edit your list mentally in advance: put down absolutely every skill you believe you have in one or other of these two columns.

Start by going back in time to your schooldays. Think of all the things you learned at school and throughout your academic life. What subjects were you naturally good at? What skills did you emerge from school with? You might find already you can enter on your sheet some or all of the following: numeracy, literacy, interpersonal communications and foreign language skills. Don't stop there! Think hard and make your list as long as possible.

Now go on to your personal life and itemise all the skills your hobbies, interests and enthusiasms have brought you. You might now be able to add skills to the list such as driving, car mechanics, computer skills, gardening, painting and decorating, art, childcare, planning and organisation.

We each tend to underestimate the range of skills we possess and overestimate the skills of others. Typically, many of our skills are dormant – by reawakening and updating them we can make ourselves more employable.

Move onto the jobs you have held. Take each one in turn. For each job, go through all of the skills you needed to do that job. What sort of skills would an employer now be asking for if they wanted to fill that kind of vacancy? Write them down, all of them. You must have had this skill, at least to some extent, to have worked successfully in that role. If the job involved organisation skills, management skills, team leadership, diplomacy, assertiveness, negotiation skills, salesmanship, problem-solving, budgeting skills or IT skills, then write them down and be as specific as you can about how you label them. Remember to include skills you learned at training courses and any on-the-job training that you were given.

When you believe you have finished your skills audit, try asking some people who know you well (such as close friends or former colleagues) what they think your main skills are. Phrase your question in a general way and be welcoming and accepting of whatever they say. Don't argue with them. If they believe you are good at something, pay them the respect that's due and thank them for holding that positive view of you.

Don't dismiss what they say. If you don't have the skill they have mentioned on your list already, then add it to the list.

Now for the most important and exciting part. By grouping skills together in different ways, you can see that your 'skill set', this collection of skills, equips you to perform a range of different jobs. You are not actually fixed to one particular role, industry or career. You are a flexible individual, capable of working in a variety of roles.

Try writing down each skill onto a separate card. You can modify a pack of playing cards for this. Then group your skills together in different ways and ask yourself 'If I was using these (three, four or five) skills together, what jobs could I do?'

Here's a simplified example. Let's suppose that Martin was formerly a Business Analyst. His skills audit revealed skills such as interviewing skills, presentation skills, analysis skills, numeracy, organisation skills and time management. Comments from Martin's partner suggested she admired him particularly because he's a self-starter with a lot of drive who plans things and makes things happen on his own initiative. She also thought he was very articulate and persuasive whenever he was putting a point across. By grouping his skills together in different ways, Martin might realise he was actually suited to several different careers:

Be flexible in your thinking. Nothing holds us back so much as our own fixed view of ourselves.

- Sales (interviewing skills + presentation skills + time-management skills + drive + persuasiveness).
- Market research (interviewing skills + numeracy + analysis skills + presentation skills).
- Maths teacher (presentation skills + numeracy + organisation skills + time management).

So what are your main skills? What else might you do with them?

4 RETRAIN FOR A NEW CAREER

In order to shift your career decisively in a different direction, you may need to retrain. The degree of retraining required may be large or small, depending on what you are seeking to do in the future.

If you look around, you may be surprised to find how much financial help is available for certain types of retraining. You may find some free or inexpensive courses (for example in basic computing skills or office skills) on offer which can help with your all-round employability. Career Development Loans (currently between £300 and £8,000), which are interest-free during the retraining period, can be obtained for a wide variety of approved retraining courses. They may also cover other course costs and some living expenses during the period of retraining. You can find information about these loans from DirectGov.

Search the Internet for relevant training courses that can help you switch into your new career. Look also for details of training courses in the trade press covering the sector you are interested in. You'll also find major public libraries provide you with access to this kind of information.

Private organisations, including leading recruitment and outplacement consultancies, can also provide coaching and careers advice to individuals. Although outplacement support is most commonly paid for by employers, private individuals can sometimes access support services directly. Some people choose to invest in their future careers by using their savings or redundancy payment to fund this kind of assistance.

Academic qualifications may lead you into a better and different career. You could go to university, as a mature student, and gain a degree which will propel you into a new job. In these days of students paying their way it won't be a cheap option, but perhaps your savings or your redundancy cheque will allow you to consider it. With a university course you will also get all of the benefits of a university lifestyle: friends, social life, arts and culture. Maybe there are worse things to do with the next three or four years! Or you might effectively 'go back to school' and do the A levels or GCSEs you never completed. Perhaps you rebelled in your teenage years against the constraints of school and never did get the qualifications you were capable of. This may have affected your confidence and prevented you from reaching the level at work you deserve. It could be time to put things right! This wouldn't mean going back to a school setting as you might choose to study at a College of Further Education, via evening classes or by Distance Learning.

Following redundancy, only a minority of people go back into the same kind of job they had before. Most people do something different.

REDUNDANCY TRANSFORMATIONS STUDY BY ALTERNATIVE FUTURES (2009)

Perhaps you just want to fulfil a lifelong ambition by studying a subject of great interest to you, something which has always been a passion. Perhaps doing a degree in art will give you the confidence to exhibit your paintings in public, and who knows where this will lead? Doing a drama degree could lead to something more than amateur dramatics. A foreign language degree might lead to a new life abroad.

You don't necessarily need to go down the usual routes for academic learning. Your life commitments may prohibit you from moving home or from certain hours of study. If so, don't reject this idea too quickly. There are many Distance Learning options. One of the UK's best kept secrets, for instance, is that the Open University is now Europe's largest university. It offers far more than just degree courses these days. Many of its courses are open to all, with no entry requirements. You may find you are able to claim credits for previous studies. The Open University is built around the principles of distance learning and flexible learning. You can study from home but also get support. You may be able to use one of the many Study Centres the Open University has all over the country – over 350 at the time of writing. It doesn't need to take years and cost a fortune. There is a range of introductory courses, open to anyone, lasting just twenty weeks and costing just over £100. You might take an introductory course in law, maths, understanding children or health for instance. Or you might do a short course such as 'Introduction to Counselling', 'Start Writing Fiction' or 'Understanding Human Nutrition'. Almost half of new Open University students receive financial support. The Open University is, of course, just one of many different educational options open to you.

Give yourself the edge over other candidates at interview by making sure your training is relevant and up to date.

If you are still in work, you may find it easier to make the break with your current employer if you tell them you've decided to fulfil a long-held ambition and go to university, rather than that you are off to work for a competitor! If you've just been made redundant, you may have two things going for you right now. You will have more time and you may have money if you received a redundancy cheque from your employer. This could be the time to improve your educational qualifications to propel yourself into a new job, or to pursue a passion.

RETRAINING FOR A NEW CAREER – A CASE STUDY

After graduating in chemistry, Robert took a job as a Research Scientist with an international chemicals company. He worked initially in the UK for a time and then was reassigned to a technical management role in Spain. However, the chemicals plant in Barcelona was sold while he was based there. Robert was made redundant and returned to the UK in 1990 to seek work.

Robert decided to give his career a boost by taking an MBA at the Cranfield School of Management. This was a significant investment but he felt confident it would lead to him finding a good job afterwards. 'I had seen another colleague with an MBA progressing really rapidly in his career and believed it would do the same for mine. I thought with an MBA I would find a good job quite easily – unfortunately, that didn't prove to be the case.' The British economy was in some difficulty in 1991 and he had a year of frustration immediately after gaining his MBA. He carried out various temporary jobs during this time. Robert realised that once again he needed to try something different: 'I decided to look closely at the types of job which were in demand and to think about retraining for those areas.'

There were a few teachers in Robert's extended family. His brother-in-law invited Robert to come down and stay for a week with the Science Department at his public school. Whilst Robert was there he was able to watch various teachers in action. 'I watched the science teachers taking lessons and thought to myself "I could do that!" I also knew there was a real shortage of science teachers in the UK at that time, which encouraged me to think this would be the right move for me.'

So Robert took a Career Development Loan and retrained again. He also considered personal coaching as he knew he didn't always come across as well at interviews as he should. After gaining his PGCE (Post Graduate Certificate of Education) he quickly found a job as a science teacher at a leading boys' school, where he progressed rapidly to become Head of Science.

The main lessons Robert learned were: 'Never give up. Consider retraining for something you'll be good at, and which is in demand. Also be brave enough to accept if you've taken a wrong turning. With hindsight, taking an MBA proved to be the wrong move for me. Don't lose sleep over it, just admit it and move on.'

5 INCREASE YOUR SKILL SET

Make yourself more employable. Invest some time (and perhaps a little money) to increase your skill set. Keep your knowledge up-to-date. The fact that you've made a big effort to do this will impress an employer.

If you are considering the Great Mid-Life Career Switch the future is going to look different for you. However, you might not yet have the full complement of skills yet to take you into your next job or to run your own business successfully.

> *The important thing is this: to be able at any moment to sacrifice what we are for what we could become.*
>
> CHARLES DUBOIS

So you need to think hard about increasing your skill set in whatever ways you can. Look around for cost-free opportunities or fully funded training. For instance, if you're considering moving in a new direction and starting up your own business, you may find a variety of free training seminars arranged by organisations such as Business Link and your bank.

Local evening classes can be an excellent and low-cost way of topping up your skills. Perhaps a foreign language or two would be helpful and look good on your CV? Maybe you need to top up your IT skills? Or perhaps some improvement in your presentation skills or assertiveness would make all the difference in your next job?

There are a variety of low-cost ways of increasing your skill set and making yourself more employable. For instance, if you network effectively, you will soon create a professional network of individuals who can support you – and you can support – through the months ahead. Try running an informal 'training exchange' with them. Here you offer to train someone else in a subject you know about if they will train you in return on their specialist subject. Someone who is experienced in using Powerpoint or Excel software might arrange to train someone who has excellent presentation skills and be trained on how to become a better presenter in return. This kind of exchange with professional contacts can apply to more than just training – you will find a professional network will benefit you in many ways.

> *In times of change learners inherit the Earth, while the learned find themselves beautifully equipped to deal with a world that no longer exists.*
>
> ERIC HOFFER

If you want to break into a new area consider this thought: why not try to 'shadow' a person who works in that field? Say that you want to break into PR and your friend's sister works in that field. Ask if you can shadow her for a day or two to understand what the job involves. You should offer to do this on an unpaid basis, of course. (And if you are currently in work you'll need to do this during a period of annual leave.) If there's an opportunity to move beyond shadowing and help actively in some way, then seize it! For instance, you might offer to take notes for her during meetings and type them up afterwards.

Voluntary work can be a way of keeping your skills up to date. Perhaps you've been out of the office environment for a while and could volunteer to help (during spare time or in the holidays) in the Head Office of a charity. The mere fact of being immersed in an office again will help refresh your skills.

Public libraries provide a practical, free way of training yourself. If you need to understand an industry before you apply for a job there, you can carry out research at a library at no cost. If you want to begin to train yourself in a new career – sales or marketing, teaching or coaching, finance or consultancy, publishing or PR, computing or catering – you can do worse than begin by reading some books on the subject. If you do decide to train yourself, do it properly. Make detailed notes as you go through the book. Type these notes up later. Talk them through with someone else. By the time you have done this, the points will have passed through your head at least three times. Read, write and recall! You will find you remember the points you have learned and can talk about them when questioned. So when you go for that job interview, you can begin to demonstrate a grasp of the subject as a result of your self-study. You can impress an employer with your initiative. You may even be able to quote from leading industry figures.

6 START YOUR OWN BUSINESS

One simple way to change career direction is to become self-employed. You don't need someone else to believe in you and offer you another job – you can start up your own business if you believe strongly enough in yourself!

If you believe you have a talent in a particular direction, then don't let anyone else stop you. Do it yourself! If your enthusiasm is great enough you will do whatever it takes to succeed. You may have worked all your life in one career, but know from your skills audit that you could use your talents in another way or apply them in a very different field. Or you may have skills and interests which you show outside of work but don't currently reveal in the workplace. These could help you make your way successfully into self-employment.

What is it that you love doing? What job would really excite and motivate you? Now could be the time to make it happen. The only thing holding you back could be yourself. One defining characteristic of successful entrepreneurs is that they are enthusiastic about what they do. They love the *business* of *business*. From Richard Branson through to Duncan Bannatyne or Stelios, serial entrepreneurs believe in themselves and what they can achieve. They are passionate in pursuit of their ambitions. If you can find a way of turning your passion into your job, you will have found yourself a new career to motivate you every single day of your life. You will have found a new career where you will be determined to succeed. You will work hard and put in long hours because it will not *feel* like work.

Sue Donnelly is a professional image coach who runs her own business, Accentuate. Sue originally ran a travel agency and has changed career direction completely, bouncing back after being made redundant twice in her life. She had a dramatic 'Eureka moment' after her first meeting with a personal image trainer. She knew, at that precise moment, that this was what she wanted to do for the rest of her life. She changed career direction completely and has never looked back.

Consider this: only a small number of British employees feel passionate about their job, yet most successful entrepreneurs are passionate about the work that they do.

The reason for Sue's success? 'What I've done in the five years since I set up on my own, I now realise, are all the things I used to love as a child. As a child I used to spend my time endlessly playing with adult dolls, dressing them up in all kinds of different outfits. Now I do the same with adults. I used to spend lots of time as a child writing stories – now I write books on personal image issues. It's as if I've tapped into a passionate vein that was running through my entire life! It doesn't feel like work, it just feels like what I was meant to do.'

Sue's passion was fashion. What's yours?

Write down on a piece of paper five things you are passionate about. Then spend fifteen minutes brainstorming with your partner or a good friend to identify ways in which you could somehow turn that passion into a job.

If you are fascinated by education and childcare, could you set up a nursery or out-of-school club?

If you love classic cars, could you run a club for enthusiasts, or run a business trading in classic cars, their spare parts or accessories?

If helping people gives you a buzz, could you become a trainer or coach?

If gardening excites you and you have an eye for colour schemes, could you run your own garden design business?

If you are an art-lover, could you run an art gallery or set up a business trading in works of art?

If you are enthusiastic about sport and health could you become a personal trainer?

While you do this exercise, suspend your disbelief. Allow yourself to believe it is possible. Don't veto each thought as soon as you have it by saying 'But I could never do that' or 'It's a nice idea but I'd never earn a living from it'. If you are passionate enough about it, you can find a way. Once you've had the idea, investigate it, try to talk to others who have done what you dream of doing. You'll find once you've spoken to people who have already made it happen, you begin to believe it could happen for you too.

Choosing the correct legal status for your business can be tricky, but there are plenty of good sources of advice.

You'll also need some help with forecasting cash flow and formulating your business plans. Talking to Business Link (a publicly funded organisation that runs free introductory seminars on starting your own business), to your bank and a small-business coach at an early stage is a wise move.

If you're starting up your own business, its legal status is something you need to sort out at the very beginning. Should you be a sole trader or form a limited company, a partnership or a limited liability partnership? If in doubt, you might always start as a sole trader and evolve your business later into another form. Talk to your small business coach or accountant about this decision.

Your bank will also be able to advise you. Banks often provide factsheets and face-to-face advice for customers who are thinking of starting their own business. Since your bank will be a crucial business partner to help you grow, it is a good idea to speak to them and seek their advice at an early stage. NatWest is a leading UK bank that is giving extra support nowadays to new business start-ups. According to NatWest, 'we've found that financial worries are the main reason customers give for not turning their idea into a business. So what we're doing is providing each new small business customer with two years' free banking and a dedicated Business Manager based at their local branch. More than 1,000 NatWest relationship managers are on hand to help startup customers in all the important areas, including managing cash flow, planning, risk management and marketing.'

Before you get moving with all this, you need to decide what your business will offer, what to call it and determine its legal status. A quick summary of the main choices available are:

- *Sole trader* – the simplest way of running a business. It consists of an individual working alone, such as a freelancer. The person *is* the business. You get to keep all the profits personally but the downside is that you are also personally liable for all debts.
- *Partnership* – two or more individuals collaborating and sharing the costs and risks of running a business. All partners register as self-employed and take a share in the profits. Creditors can make a claim against any of the partners. So you really are in it together!
- *Limited company* – a company such as XYZ Ltd that exists as a separate legal entity in its own right and where the company's finances are separate from the personal finances of the company's owners. Shareholders are not normally responsible for the company's debts. The company can be bought and sold. Limited companies need to be registered at Companies House.
- *Limited liability partnership* – a company such as XYZ LLP, similar to an ordinary partnership in that a number of individuals together share in the risks and rewards. However, the liability is limited, so that members have some protection if the business runs into trouble.

It's not inevitable that if you are operating alone you should set up as a sole trader. Sometimes you might operate alone on a day-to-day basis, but still choose to set up a limited company. You are legally obliged, though, to have someone else acting as your Company Secretary.

According to a recent survey by One Life Live, 43 per cent of Britons dream of starting their own business. Nowadays that dream is as likely to be starting an IT consultancy business or a creative design agency as running a shop. Britain is no longer just a nation of shopkeepers! What kind of business might you start?

7 BUY A BUSINESS FRANCHISE

If you want to be your own boss and have money to invest, the easiest way to get started may be to buy a business franchise. You operate under an established brand or company name, using a proven business model. And you get to run it yourself – although you'll find you have to work to set procedures and standards set out in the franchise agreement.

Got the get-up-and-go to be your own boss? Do you have savings you could invest in making this change of career? Have you received a large redundancy cheque from your former employer that would otherwise get frittered away over the next year or two? Are you keen to take up a new challenge, to do something different right now? Do you like the idea of running your own business but you're still not sure what and would feel uncertain about doing it alone?

A business franchise could be the answer. There are thousands of franchise opportunities available. Franchise owners are always looking to expand their businesses by bringing in new managers to run franchise operations. Some of the biggest brand names are actually franchise operations. The most famous franchise of all is probably McDonald's restaurants, although managing a McDonald's restaurant wouldn't be for everyone. Other famous franchises include ActionCoach (business coaching), Bairstow Eves (estate agents), Cartridge World (printing refills), Chips-Away (car repairs), Coffee Republic (coffee shops), Clarks (retailer of shoes), Domino's Pizza (takeaway), Kall Kwik (printing), Molly Maid (cleaning), Pitman Training (training colleges for office skills), Rosemary

Conley (diet and fitness clubs), Scottish & Newcastle (pubs), Stagecoach (theatre schools), TaxAssist (accountants) and Western Provident Association (medical insurance). There are franchise operations covering just about every business sector you might want to get into!

Banks are more likely to lend to you as a franchisee than for a small business idea you have developed yourself. This is because as a franchisee you are working to a well-defined, proven business model. They know you can be successful because that business model has a proven track record of success. The franchisor will give you examples of what you can hope to earn and introduce you to people who are running their existing franchises successfully.

As a general rule you'll need *at least* £20,000 (sometimes significantly more for retail-based franchises) to invest in a franchise. This payment will cover your initial franchise fee. This money pays for you to buy the licence to operate under that brand for a particular length of time, for instance five years. There will probably be geographical restrictions on your franchise: you might be buying the right to operate under that brand in a particular town or region of the country, for instance. The cost of franchises varies significantly and there are a few franchises (often for home-based roles) that cost a great deal less than this. You'll also have ongoing management services charges to pay: typically you pay the franchisor a specified percentage of your turnover. You may be bound by your contract to purchase all supplies in future from the franchisor, for example if you are running a restaurant or a coffee shop.

Banks will be more likely to lend to you as a franchisee than for a small business idea you've developed yourself, because a franchisee is operating a proven business model.

In return, you will get to operate under an established brand that is being supported by central advertising and promotional activity. You'll receive comprehensive training plus ongoing management support. You may get support for central services such as finance or HR, so you're not hassled by invoicing or employee contracts.

Of course, in the first instance you need to be accepted by the franchisor as a suitable person to run a franchise for their brand. They will have quality control measures in place to ensure you fulfil your side of the bargain and don't damage their brand. Just because you have the money to do it, you can't assume you will be accepted to run a franchise. But there are hundreds of franchises out there to be run. Franchisors want to find people who have management expertise, motivation and money to invest. They want to expand their businesses by bringing in new people like you! Since you are paying for the franchise, the balance of power is certainly different from an employer-employee relationship. You're not asking them to give you a job, you're investing in a business opportunity with them as your business partner.

What's the downside? Well, obviously the cost can be a big barrier. Be sure you understand the ongoing cash requirements of the business and don't make the common mistake of underestimating these. Buying a franchise is not a move to be taken lightly. You need to do careful research first. For those of a creative bent, the restrictions and quality control measures in the franchise agreement can be a challenge. You won't have the freedom to innovate that would come from having created your own business. You need to follow fixed processes and procedures. It's also a significant tie: you are committing to doing this for a specified period. Be sure you understand the exit routes before you walk in the entry door.

If you think franchising appeals to you, the best first steps are to:

- read a magazine such as *FranchiseWorld* or *The Franchise Magazine*
- check out various franchising websites such as the British Franchise Association (the BFA also runs low-cost seminars about franchising)
- visit a franchising exhibition such as the British and International Franchise Exhibition, and speak to experts on franchising.

Make sure that you've spoken to several people who are already part of the franchise network for that business before you commit to taking one up. Understand the practical challenges you are likely to face. It will be hard work. You will need to be determined and committed to make it work. However, for some, this chance to run a business using an established brand, a proven business model and with central training and support, will be exactly what they want.

8 GIVE YOURSELF A FRESH IMAGE

The image you convey is incredibly important. Whether you are hoping to shine at a job interview or you are starting up your own business and trying to win clients, you need to project the right image.

Take a good look at yourself in the mirror. It may be time for a new look, a new image – a new you!

Here's a thought. At a job interview your prospective employers will typically have made up their mind about you within five minutes of your arrival. They'll do so on the basis of both verbal and non-verbal communication. As everyone has probably heard by now, more than 90% of all communication is non-verbal. Your appearance, your body language and your clothes are all sending messages to others about you.

'Communication is 55% appearance, 38% tone, 7% words.'
ALBERT MEHRABIAN, THE SILENT REPORT

Even when employers weigh up your answers to interview questions, how you said it could be as important as what you said. So you do need to think about your tone of voice, the confidence with which you speak, the clarity and pace of what you say.

Image is a double influence. The way you look will affect how people react to you and also affect how confident you feel when you speak. In your last or current career you may have developed a particular image. That image may have been entirely appropriate for that job but it will not necessarily be the right one to help you succeed in your new career. Your new career may call for a different image – a new you.

Leading image coach Sue Donnelly is President of the Federation of Image Consultants. She also runs her own image consultancy, Accentuate. Her view on personal image is that 'it should be the first thing people think about if they want to relaunch themselves – nothing is more important when it comes to increasing your self-confidence'.

Sue herself bounced back from redundancy (she has been made redundant twice in her career) when she finally discovered her niche and set up her own image consultancy business. She is now a published author, with books such as *Feel Fab at Fifty*, is a regular conference speaker and is author of numerous magazine articles on personal image and impact.

You won't win a job purely by the way you look, but you may lose it!

Here's Sue's advice. 'If you're going for a job interview, be aware that first impressions matter enormously. The way you dress needs to communicate your personality. Take care of the small as well as the large details. Make sure your hair is styled to suit you, that your shoes aren't scuffed and that your fingernails are neat. You need to dress for your audience expectations, but you also need to be authentic. If the two don't match up, then you really do need to think whether you're right for the job!

'A new outfit for an interview will obviously lift your spirits – but make sure you choose it yourself and you feel good in it. You should have already worn the outfit a couple of times so that you feel comfortable and relaxed in it. You can then concentrate on the job in hand rather than your clothes.

'Think also about whether your clothes communicate that you are powerful or approachable. In general, approachability is going to be communicated by more colourful outfits, greater use of patterns and softer fabrics. Power is communicated by more sober outfits that use fewer colours and patterns. What message do you want your audience to receive?'

If you can look the part on arrival at interview, you've crossed the first hurdle.

Think about what you'd like a prospective employer to be saying about you after your job interview. Then ask a trusted friend what your clothes and appearance say about you. Encourage them to be totally honest and forthright. If the employer wants someone who is self-confident, personable, opinionated and a go-getter, but your clothes and appearance are shouting 'Quiet, conservative, shy', then you simply aren't going to get that job.

For men this can be a particularly difficult point to take on board. Many men, particularly those who've been with a single employer for a long time, may have stopped thinking too hard about the suit they put on every morning, or their overall look. They may have stopped thinking about the image they convey through the way they dress. Any steps they take to lift their image will pay dividends in raising their confidence.

9 BE FOCUSED

The greater clarity you can have about your goal, the more successful you will be. If you can achieve clarity then you can visualise success. You can focus.

Top athletes will use one word repeatedly in interviews. That word is 'focus'. With focus comes drive and determination. They have clarity of purpose. Diversionary activities that clutter their lives and don't contribute to their main goal can be avoided.

No one gets to be a top athlete without dedication. Hours of practice, day after day. Whether they feel in the mood or not. Whether they feel on top form or not. Every day, top athletes will follow their daily training regime. What helps them maintain their motivation through all of this is their focus. They have a strong vision of the end goal. Perhaps their aim is to win a gold medal at the Olympics, or to represent their country at a particular event, or simply to achieve a personal best at a particular athletics event. The goal is clear. It is tangible and time-limited. It can be easily visualised. All of this helps to increase focus. Ask yourself: would an athlete without focus be successful?

> *'Nothing can add more power to your life than concentrating all of your energies on a limited set of targets.'*
> NIDO QUBEIN, MOTIVATIONAL SPEAKER

So how can you be focused right now?

At the moment you may have a myriad of future possibilities swirling around in your mind. Should you retrain? Should you look for an interim position? Should you start your own business or invest in a business franchise? There are many future directions you might take and at this moment you might not know which one will be the best route to take.

Here's a suggestion. Begin by drawing up a simple four-point schedule. The timings must be based on what you know about your practical situation, for instance your financial situation. You've worked out how long your money will last and you know you need to make things happen within that timeframe.

1 Point 1 on your schedule might be labelled 'Thinking time'. You might choose to give yourself a few months for this, depending on your situation. During this period you will take time to think through your situation, take stock of your options, talk to trusted friends and colleagues, meet with professional advisers, and research other careers and possibilities.

2 Point 2 on your schedule could be labelled 'Determine direction'. This is your moment of choice. The time you decide on your goal. The direction you are now going to select, from amongst all of your options. Choose well. Don't leap to a choice too early, but don't delay making that choice simply because you are afraid to.

3 Point 3 on your schedule could read 'Making it happen'. List the actions you will take to move towards that goal. Other than generic actions, such as networking, this section will be largely blank at first until your goal has been determined. You can begin to fill in the detail against this point in the schedule as your future direction becomes clearer.

4 Point 4, the final entry on your schedule, could be labelled 'Arrival'. When do you need to have arrived at your destination? Working back from this, what timings do you need to have against points 1, 2 and 3?

See if you can create in your mind, as early as possible, an image of yourself at this arrival point in the future. There you are, actually doing this job. If your goal is to retrain as a teacher, you might see an image of yourself standing in the classroom, addressing the students. Hold that picture in your mind as firmly as possible. Try to imagine what it would feel like, what sort of thing you might say, so that your image is as complete as possible.

Great buildings are created twice; once in the imagination and once in practice. An architect will prepare detailed technical drawings of the building before it is built. No great building could be created without this kind of vision in advance, a clear picture of what it will ultimately look like. Could the Pyramids, the Eiffel Tower, the Taj Mahal or St Paul's Cathedral have been built without a plan, without a vision?

You may need to be patient in achieving that vision. If you are currently in work and not enjoying the job you do you may find it quite hard to be patient. You will benefit, however, from thinking things through before you act. If you've been made redundant, on the other hand, and have no job, you will find it even harder to be patient. Yet patience is what is required! Research by Alternative Futures shows that following redundancy one in four people find a new job straight away, within a month of redundancy, but that the same number are still looking for a job or have entered early retirement over a year later. If you are looking to change career direction it may not be possible for this change to happen straight away. Half of those who have experienced redundancy say it is important not to just take the first job you are offered. If you've recently been made redundant you will need to have a clear resolve if you are to be that strong!

'I can give you a six-word formula for success: "Think things through then follow through".'
EDDIE RICKENBACKER, EARLY 20TH CENTURY MOTOR RACER AND FIGHTER PILOT

You want to achieve great things in your life and so you need a vision too. If you can create a strong, compelling vision of yourself in a new job role, you can begin to make it happen. You will have a clarity of focus. Stephen Covey picked this out as being one of the seven habits of highly effective people. They 'begin with the end in mind'. With that focus comes determination to succeed. Be focused on a clear goal and you will be more successful at attaining it.

10 NETWORK TO DEVELOP YOUR CONNECTIONS

Networking with friends, former working colleagues and relatives could help you make your career switch. You will also find it useful to make totally new connections.

If you are going to achieve this change in your life it will be essential to stay active and connect with others. In some cases, this word should perhaps be 'reconnect'. Look up your old friends again – seek out some of your more distant relatives and acquaintances that you haven't had time to see for a long while. Social networking websites can help you do this. There are many good networking websites around like Friends Reunited (for old school friends) and LinkedIn or Plaxo (for previous work colleagues, helping you find out where they are now so you can get back in contact). Every contact you make will inevitably throw up an 'Are you still in contact with Paul or Kate?' moment. Have they heard what a former colleague is doing these days? This kind of discussion can lead to reconnections with people you'd lost touch with. Each expansion of your contact pool may bring you closer to your next job. Meeting up with old contacts can also be a lot of fun along the way!

Networking helps you to take the initiative in your life. You can make job opportunities happen!

Your friends and relatives can help you to find a new job. They can be your 'eyes and ears' everywhere they go. It's an obvious thing to say but to get a new job you need to hear about it and a prospective employer needs to hear about you. That employer is more likely to take a chance on you if you come recommended to them by a trusted member of their staff (your friend or relative). We've all heard the adage 'it's not what you know, it's who you know' that gets you into a job. That is particularly the case when you're changing careers and the job you are seeking is not one which your past experience naturally suggests you for.

'One person in every four finds their next job following redundancy via networking. For senior managers, this figure rises to one in three.'

REDUNDANCY TRANSFORMATIONS
STUDY, ALTERNATIVE FUTURES, 2009

Consider this for a moment: Think of those among your good friends or close relatives who are in a job at the moment. Think of the organisations that employ them. How many employers does that give you some kind of a connection with? Let's say the answer is fifty. If your friends and relatives stay alert on your behalf, they can tip you off about any jobs that are going with the companies they work for. So you have perhaps fifty employers 'under surveillance'. For these fifty employers you would hope to hear quickly about any new job opportunities for which you were suitable.

But let's assume your friends and relatives are even more active than that. As a result of speaking to you they are fully informed and energised on your behalf. They are now actively looking for new opportunities for you. Because they've spoken recently to you they know exactly what kind of new job you are looking for, that you're looking to do something different from the job you were doing before. So they don't just keep tabs on job opportunities with their own employer, they also talk about you and your career shifting situation to all their friends. Whenever they get the chance, they talk about you and mention the kind of job you are looking for. Now how many connections do you have? You won't just connect with your friends' employers but the employers of everyone they know. Do the maths. Now you might have indirect connections with 50×50 = 2500 employers. If you network actively, you can potentially be alerted about job opportunities with several thousand different employers.

Many of the job opportunities you will hear about via networking are never advertised.

Making totally new connections is very important too. This doesn't have to be a complete cold call. If someone you know offers to introduce you to someone who they think can help you, go along with this. Take up their kind offer and make that connection happen! If you are thinking of starting up your own business, for instance, there are many networking events you can attend. In the early days of considering whether or not to become self-employed, you'll probably be meeting like-minded people at seminars run by Business Link or your bank. Most major towns have a variety of breakfast, lunch and evening networking gatherings for the business community. These are organised by everyone from the local Chamber of Commerce and professional bodies through to commercial networking organisations like BNI (Business Network International) or BRX (Business Referral Exchange). Some networking organisations organise for members to meet locally once a week, over a meal, and swap contacts. It's the 'you help me and I'll help you in return' principle. You can usually attend one meeting initially as a non-member. You may not even have started your own business formally yet (for instance you might simply be looking for some freelance work as a way into your new career) but you can still go along to these kinds of meetings. Some mistakenly expect them to be formal, intimidating affairs. They aren't, they're just another way of making connections. Look to help the people you encounter. If you can do someone else a favour, they may return the favour. You will generally find, as a rule of thumb, that you need to meet someone face-to-face on at least three occasions to begin to establish that person as a helpful networking contact. They won't instantly feel comfortable enough with you or familiar enough with your experience to refer you to others. So don't expect instant results. You have to work hard to develop mutual understanding and trust.

When you're looking to make your Great Mid-Life Career Switch, you may need some help and a little luck to get your first job in your new career. Many people are initially cynical about the idea of building and maintaining a professional network. But one of the main assets you have built up during all of your working life to this point is a pool of contacts who you know and trust, and who know and trust you. Make sure you use this asset. Networking works! Make sure it works for you.

11 FIND INSPIRATION

Feed your motivation. Look for inspiration by visiting inspirational events, reading books that will be uplifting and listening to CDs by motivational speakers.

Stephen Covey, Susan Jeffers, Zig Ziglar, Anthony Robbins, Edward de Bono and many others can help you out of the place in which you find yourself right now.

They are inspirational authors and speakers who can help you look at your life and the challenges facing you in a different way. There is an array of self-help literature out there to help sustain you through the days ahead. If you make a point of reading it, or listening to it, some of it will strike a chord within you. That's almost certain. It is practically impossible to read or listen to these individuals without feeling energised and motivated by some of their words.

'You can have everything in life if you will just help others to get what they want.'
ZIG ZIGLAR , MOTIVATIONAL AUTHOR AND SPEAKER

When I set up my own business eight years ago, I found the following authors and their works particularly uplifting. I used the evenings to read books and the car journeys to listen to tapes, to help me absorb some of the lessons. I can thoroughly recommend each of the following:

- **Stephen Covey's *The Seven Habits of Highly Effective People*.** If you come out of reading this book adopting even one of the seven habits, you'll be a better person. Take for example Habit Number 1, 'Be proactive'. If you can make things happen, by networking and making contacts, by doing favours for other people that they will repay, then you can create opportunities for yourself. Or Habit Number 2, 'Begin with the end in mind': if you can create a clear vision of the job you want or the business you want to create, you're well on the way to getting there.

- **Susan Jeffers' *Feel the Fear and Do It Anyway*.** This book underlines the thought that brave people aren't those without any fear – they are people who don't allow their fear to stop them from doing what they want to do. You might be afraid now, about retraining and taking your career in a completely new direction or about whether or not you've got what it takes to be successfully self-employed. But don't let the fear stop you. Feel the fear and do it anyway.

- **Zig Ziglar's *Five Steps to Successful Selling* (audiobook).** For those who are starting up their own business, sales skills are going to be very important. You may be technically proficient and so may be able to follow the processes and do the technical work to a very high standard, but how will you make the sale in the first place? How do you prospect for sales and convince someone else to buy from you? Equally, if you are going for job interviews, you need to learn to 'sell yourself' persuasively at interview. Zig Ziglar is someone who helps you see the simple principles of selling and underlines how you can get what you want in life by helping other people get what they want. Stephen Covey makes a similar kind of point: Habit Number 6 of highly effective people is 'Seek first to understand, then to be understood'. One of the principles of successful salesmanship is to get the customer to talk about their needs and then explain how what you are offering will help answer their needs.

Find some authors whose words will motivate you.

Use spare moments each day to read self-help literature and practical books. They will help you to take your next steps and set you on the stairs that lead upwards. Seek out books on effective networking, interview technique, running your own business, life coaching, assertiveness, career development or whatever areas you feel you are most in need of support.

Get out to visit events that will give you ideas and motivate you. There are many free or low-cost exhibitions and seminars that can provide a fund of ideas. One such event, which is held in London every spring, is the One Life Live exhibition. Here, under one roof, you will find organisations that can help you with major life changes such as starting your own business, volunteering, retraining for a new career, emigration and international travel. The One Life Live exhibition also runs a series of workshops with motivational speakers in parallel with the exhibition itself. Look out for this kind of event and other events that are close to you. You will emerge energised and enthused.

'Undoubtedly, we become what we envisage.'

CLAUDE M. BRISTOL, SELF-HELP AUTHOR

At this time in your life you need to surround yourself with positive influences. You need to listen to positive voices, people who believe things can happen rather than those who wallow in their own pessimism and pour cold water on the hopes of others. Seek out the company of people you know and admire. If there is a former colleague or old friend you admire but you've lost touch with, try to find out where they are now and meet up again. If you are considering launching your own business, find someone to speak to who has done it themselves and is successful. If you are thinking of moving into a different career, find someone who is successful in that career to speak to. Seek out people you admire, tell them how much you admire them, and ask them the secret of their success. You are likely to find them willing to share their experiences with you.

Be inspired!

12 TAKE VOLUNTARY WORK

Voluntary work is not just a way of keeping your mind and body active, or an opportunity to do some good in this world and make yourself feel better. It can also lead you to make important new connections and even into a new career.

Some of you reading this book will still be in full-time work, while others will have just experienced redundancy. If you find yourself with time on your hands following redundancy, there are some very simple *dos* and *don'ts* to observe. Observing them, however, requires a strong degree of self-discipline:

- Don't oversleep: long lie-ins will leave you feeling lethargic and dispirited.
- Do keep active.
- Don't waste your days watching daytime TV.
- Do get out and meet people.
- Don't be self-critical.
- Do give yourself praise where it is due.

Voluntary work is a good way to make sure you tick off some of the *dos* on your list and avoid some of the *don'ts*. It does many things for you all at once: it feeds your self-esteem, it keeps you active and it gets you out into the world where you can make new contacts. If you are able to use your professional skill – if you're an IT professional and you offer to help a local charity to develop the IT skills of their office staff, for example – then you can keep your experience up to date. You can use the act of volunteering to keep your hand in. Perhaps you can even spot an opportunity to volunteer for something that will expand your skill set? If you are in work, you might still see opportunities for voluntary work in the evenings or weekends which will help with your intended Career Switch. For instance, if you are thinking of making a career move from the private sector into the public sector, some appropriate voluntary activities in your spare time could enhance your CV.

'The best way to cheer yourself up is to cheer somebody else up.'
MARK TWAIN

Voluntary work might show you a path into a new career. After all, there is more to life than making money. You may find working in the not-for-profit sector sparks something off in you that you really hadn't expected. You may suddenly realise you'd like to work in this sector and discover exactly how you might make a worthwhile contribution. Even if it doesn't set off a desire to work in the sector, you will be making contacts through your voluntary work. Any one of these contacts could be a good networking contact for you. Networking is not necessarily about whether the person you are talking to can help you, but whether they know someone who can help you. All networking contacts can be promising contacts.

VOLUNTEERING – A CASE STUDY

Here's the story of how Tony went from a commercial career to be a project co-ordinator for a major national charity.

Tony had been working as a customer support manager in the aerospace industry. After twenty-five years with his employer, he found himself being made redundant when the company was involved in a merger and his role was duplicated in the other organisation. It wasn't a good time to be looking for another job in this sector. 'So many other people in the industry were in exactly the same position as me,' he explains. He spent eight months looking for jobs and was having no luck whatsoever. 'At the time I was only getting around

20% of my letters answered. I was starting to feel quite despondent when a chance occurrence changed my life. A friend of mine had recently lost her husband. She'd been invited (there was an announcement at her church) to go along to a Volunteers Day that was being held by a charity. The charity wanted to talk to people who might be persuaded to volunteer. They wanted to talk to them over tea and biscuits, and show them different ways they might help. My friend didn't want to go on her own. She knew I'd do anything for a cup of tea and a biscuit, so she asked me if I'd go along with her.'

Tony's friend never did find any voluntary work with the charity that she could fit in with her other commitments, but Tony did. 'A couple of days later, I was phoned up by the Volunteers Co-ordinator for the charity, to see if I could help with some administrative work in the Membership Department. At first I was working as a volunteer on one afternoon a week, though it quickly went up to two afternoons. Just doing basic admin really – answering letters, taking phone calls, that sort of thing. After about six months a contract job came up with the charity to do administrative work on a paid basis. They asked me if I'd like to do it. The contract was then extended to twelve months.'

After a brief break back in the commercial world, Tony is now back working in a full-time role with the same charity as a project co-ordinator in the Youth and Education Department. He says this of the shift which has taken place in his working life. 'I'm happier than I was at the end of my aerospace career, for sure. It's not a rat race here! I work with a lovely bunch of people and I enjoy going to work each day. I have a much better work-life balance than I had previously.'

Could the act of volunteering help your life take a new direction?

13 USE AN INTERIM POSITION AS A STEPPING STONE

You want a permanent full-time job in your new career, don't you? So why would you accept a temporary or part-time job? Why choose interim management, holiday or maternity cover, or a short-term contract rather than seek a longer-term role? The answer is simple: because it can be a stepping stone that helps you on towards your real goal.

Following a global recession, employers are understandably going to be nervous. Companies big and small will be more risk-averse. They don't want to take on anyone they can't really afford, who might not turn out to be the right person for the job.

So we're seeing fewer full-time permanent jobs and more part-time, temporary jobs and short-term contracts. We're also seeing greater emphasis on outsourcing and the use of a flexible workforce of freelancers. However, companies may see employing someone on a short-term or contract basis as a good way of assessing them. If you can impress, this temporary opportunity could lead on to a permanent position. Part-time work could lead on to a full-time job.

It's easier to win a new job in an organisation from inside. If a company is downsizing and cutting down on external recruitment, it may not even advertise a new position externally. You may get to hear about it from your position on the inside. Even if the company plans to advertise the position externally, you may hear about it before they have done so. If it's a job you are qualified to do, you could save that company the cost of

Your journey to your new career may be like a long train journey. It may go via some interesting places. Be prepared to take a long route with many stops rather than expecting to travel direct to your destination.

external advertising and a drawn-out recruitment process by quickly having a word with the right manager in that company. However, you do need to act quickly and be bold!

You can also use short-term or interim work as a way of keeping your skill set up to date, refreshing skills you haven't used for a while or gaining experience of a new industry. All of these might be important factors in helping you towards the job you really want.

Importantly you can also combine a significant period of retraining with temporary employment to build your credentials for that new career. You might for instance go to university for three years to retrain in a new career direction, but use your holidays to do temporary or interim work which will help towards your new career.

14 CREATE A PORTFOLIO CAREER

At the moment you're probably thinking about finding one new job. But the right solution for you could be something completely different, such as two part-time jobs that taken together provide the income you need. Or a part-time role coupled with freelancing activities. Be open to all the possibilities.

The world of work is changing. The old model of employment – mainly full-time, permanent jobs stationed at a fixed workplace – no longer applies in all cases. Employers may seek more flexible mobile workforces featuring a different mix of permanent, part-time and predominantly home-based contract staff.

More than twenty years ago the management guru Charles Handy looked at the future of working practices and predicted that in the twenty-first century, more than 50% of jobs would be something other than full-time. He foresaw a growing number of part-time, flexitime, temporary and self-employment options being used. With the impetus to change employment practices provided by a global recession, perhaps we are about to see Charles Handy's vision becoming the reality?

Two jobs may be better than one – and easier to find.

If you used to be a manager in an industry that has suffered from the economic downturn, it may be very hard for you to find a like-for-like swap. It may be very difficult to find another full-time permanent job just like your last one. Funnily enough, it might be easier for you to find two jobs (part-time or short-term) than one.

Your 'Monday to Friday 9 to 5' may be about to become your 'Monday to Wednesday 9 to 5 and Thursday to Friday 12 to 6', only with two different employers. What's wrong with that? Variety is the spice of life. You may enjoy having a greater variety of work, even if it requires more planning to juggle your family commitments. The two jobs option does not necessarily imply deterioration in your work-life balance. It may mean living on less income, but not necessarily.

Clearly, a portfolio career, where you combine several different jobs at once, has its attractions. Daniel Gilbert, the author of the best-selling book *Stumbling on Happiness*, believes the best way for you to find out what will make you happy is to try it. A portfolio career will give you the chance to try out two or three types of work, all at the same time!

Certain fields such as academia or the arts, lend themselves naturally to portfolio careers. Lecturer plus writer and non-executive director, perhaps? Some industries, such as farming, have been practising portfolio careers for years, although in agriculture they call it 'diversification'. I well remember taking my family on holiday on a farm when my children were young. The attraction of this particular holiday was that the farmer allowed the young children to get involved with feeding the animals at feeding time. Both my son and daughter loved animals. The farmer not only ran his agricultural smallholding, with its farm shop and bed & breakfast, he also worked part-time as a graphic designer. He had a true portfolio career!

Here are a few thoughts. One of them might strike a chord with you. Why not try to combine a morning-only part-time job with working as a freelancer in the afternoons or evenings? Why not teach an evening class while working elsewhere in the mornings or afternoons? Why not set up your own sole trader business with the target of earning just half your previous earnings and look for a part-time job or contract job to make up the income gap?

Perhaps you also know enough about certain subjects to teach others about them or write about them, and could do this alongside another job. Perhaps a private passion (such as collecting antiques, paintings, jewellery or classic cars) could become the basis for your own part-time small business that you run alongside another job.

Perhaps the question you should be asking yourself right now is, what *combination of careers* would bring in sufficient money and also keep you happy?

15   BELIEVE IN YOURSELF!

Whichever route you choose you should believe that your life is going to be better in future, not worse. Your current situation is a call to action, a challenge to see how you will respond. Everything is possible if first you believe in yourself.

Don't make the mistake of defining your own value as a person in terms of work. As David D. Burns succinctly put it, 'your work is not your worth'. You are far more than that. You are capable of much more.

There is a study of success that is known as NLP: neuro-linguistic programming to give it its full title, though this can sound rather academic and off-putting. NLP was developed in the USA by a maths undergraduate, Richard Bandler, who had an interest in computing and psychology, working with Dr John Grinder, an Associate Professor of linguistics. It was Bandler and Grinder who first proposed trying to replicate the results of another person by modelling their behaviours and methods.

The conclusions they arrived at are far-reaching. Bandler and Grinder proposed that if one person can do something, someone else can learn to do it by emulating their thinking and behaviour. So you (yes, you!), if you really wanted to, could learn to think and behave like a successful entrepreneur, an inspirational teacher or a selfless campaigner for charitable causes – or someone else you greatly admire.

But first you must believe in yourself! If you begin by saying to yourself 'They are much better people than me, I couldn't hope to be as successful as them' or 'I could never do that!' then you never will – that much is certain. If you think you are beaten, you are. However, if you believe in yourself and follow the instruction of Ella Wheeler Wilcox to 'trust in your own untried capacity', you can aim much higher than the level you are at today.

If you are to emulate the success of others, the first thing you need to do is to get closer to them. Try to understand the way they think. Try to understand the way they act. If you want to become a successful entrepreneur like Duncan Bannatyne or Richard Branson, begin by reading their autobiographies. Read press articles about their lives. Research the way they think and the decisions they take. Try to absorb their mindset and follow their lead. Imagine the same for yourself. You may yet become the person you envisage.

If you can achieve even a fraction of their success, you will be very successful indeed!

Perhaps your definition of success is somewhat different. Perhaps the person you admire most is someone a little closer to home: a relative or an old school-friend who works in a different field from you and has gone on to achieve success. By 'success', I mean success *in your view*, however you choose to define it. This may or may not involve material success – perhaps they have a lifestyle that you admire, or an alternative outlook or opinions that inspire you.

Change will not come if we wait for some other person or some other time. We are the ones we've been waiting for. We are the change that we seek.
BARACK OBAMA

Your first step should be to believe in yourself: you too could do what they have done. Your second step should be to talk to the person you admire. Tell them how much you admire them and why. Ask them to tell you the story of how they have achieved all the things they have achieved. As they talk, make note of the way they thought at each key moment in their lives and the actions they took. Look particularly closely at how they handled obstacles or setbacks in their lives. Did they ever suffer redundancy or something similar – and if so, what did they do? You should seek to emulate them. Did they ever make a dramatic switch of careers? You should seek to emulate them. How would they react if they were in your shoes right now?

Imitation really is the sincerest form of flattery!

'Many a man is building for himself in his imagination a bungalow, when he should be building a palace.'
FLORENCE SCOVELL SHINN , SELF HELP WRITER

Here's how Anthony Robbins, the successful author and motivational speaker, puts it. 'Often we are caught in a mental trap of seeing enormously successful people and thinking they are where they are because they have some special gift. Yet a closer look shows that the greatest gift that extraordinarily successful people have over the average person is their ability to get themselves to take action.'

Your Great Mid-Life Career Switch may be prompted by a number of things. Perhaps you have just experienced redundancy. If so you should realise just how commonplace this experience is. Redundancy is the fifth most common Pivot Point that people experience in their lives, according to research by Alternative Futures. Along with marriage, divorce, the birth of children and the death of loved ones, redundancy is the other main turning point people commonly experience in their lives. This moment, containing the experience of redundancy, is a time when *your* life might turn around completely.

Remember that two out of every three people whose life is changed by redundancy will actually see their lives transformed *positively*. Resolve to be one of the people for whom life gets better. The same research shows that 86% of those whose lives changed for the better said that redundancy provided the spur for them to make major changes in their lives. Don't be afraid of change.

What changes do you want to make in your life?

You can make the changes that are needed but first you must believe in yourself. As Henry Ford once said, 'if you think you can or think you can't, you're probably right'. Your future can be bright. Believe in yourself and start to build it.

USEFUL CONTACTS

ONE LIFE

Annual exhibition to help individuals who are looking to make major
life changes.

www.onelifelive.co.uk

BUSINESS LINK

Free advice, workshops and seminars for people wanting to start up their
own business.

www.businesslink.gov.uk

CAREERS ADVICE SERVICE

Free careers advice and training course search.

www.careersadvice.direct.gov.uk

JOBCENTRE PLUS

Help on getting back to work and advice on benefits/entitlements.

www.jobcentreplus.gov.uk

DIRECTGOV

Website giving information about all government support and services
including training and education, career development loans, employment and mortgage debt advice.

www.direct.gov.uk

OVERCOMING REDUNDANCY
New website to help those affected by redundancy.

www.overcoming-redundancy.com

INFINITE IDEAS
Leading publisher of self-help books including the 52 Brilliant Ideas series.

www.infideas.com

BRITISH FRANCHISE ASSOCIATION
Information about franchising.

www.thebfa.org

TIME BANKING
Exchange an hour of your time for an hour of someone else's.

www.timebanking.org

THE COACHING ACADEMY
The UK's largest school for coaches.

www.the-coaching-academy.com

OPEN UNIVERSITY
The UK's only university dedicated to providing distance learning.

www.open.ac.uk

OTHER HELPFUL BOOKS FROM INFINITE IDEAS

High impact CVs:
52 brilliant ideas for making your résumé sensational
John Middleton

Knockout interview answers:
52 brilliant ideas to make job hunting a piece of cake
Ken Langdon and Nikki Cartwright

Cultivate a cool career:
52 brilliant ideas for reaching the top
Ken Langdon

Networking: work your contacts to supercharge your career
Nicolas King

Sort out your money: the only personal finance book you need to get you through the recession
Ken Langdon and John Middleton

Be your own best life coach: take charge and live the life you always wanted
Jackee Holder